Fun with Engl

Bloomers & Blunders

How to pronounce English

Norman Barrett
Illustrated by Peter Stevenson

Chambers

Editor: John Grisewood

Illustrations: Peter Stevenson
(Kathy Jakeman Illustration)

CHAMBERS
An imprint of Larousse plc
Elsley House, 24-30 Great Titchfield Street,
London W1P 7AD

First published by Chambers 1995

2 4 6 8 10 9 7 5 3 1

Illustrations copyright © Larousse plc 1995
Text © Norman Barrett 1995

All rights reserved. No part of this publication may be reproduced, stored in a retrieval system or transmitted by any means, electronic, mechanical, photocopying or otherwise, without the prior permission of the publisher.

A CIP catalogue record for this book is available from the British Library.

ISBN 0 550 32508 5

Printed in Spain

Contents

1 A little learning can lead to the ultimate detergent (*Malapropisms*)   4

2 Oops, I'll say that again (*Pronunciation*)   6

3 Don't mention the wart! (*Slips of the tongue*)   14

4 The cat that popped on its drawers (*Spoonerisms*)   15

5 Statements that don't follow (*Non sequiturs*)   17

6 What a big let-down (*Anticlimax*)   20

7 So what — it's quite meaningless! (*Weasel words*)   21

8 That's not what I meant (*Idioms*)   22

9 Sounds the same to me! (*Homophones*)   23

Answers   24

MALAPROPISMS

1 A little learning can lead to the ultimate detergent

You may have heard of the proverb 'A little learning is a dangerous thing'. It means that people who know just a little about something, but think they know it all, often make silly mistakes. This is particularly true of people who regularly use the wrong word. The use of a word in mistake for one that sounds like it is called a 'malapropism'.

We all might use a wrong word from time to time, but some people make a habit of it. They think they know the right word, but they use a similar sounding word instead.

Here is an example: 'The threat of nuclear war is the ultimate detergent.' This does not make sense, because a detergent is a cleaning powder or liquid that we use in the home. The word should be 'deterrent', something that 'deters', or puts people off doing something.

The word 'malapropism' comes from Mrs Malaprop, a character in *The Rivals*, a play by Thomas Sheridan. Her name was made up from a French word meaning 'not right' or 'out of place'.

The sort of thing Mrs Malaprop says in the play is: 'He is the very pineapple of politeness.' She meant to say that he is the very pinnacle [height] of politeness. Other utterances of hers include: 'She's as headstrong as an *allegory* on the banks of the Nile,' and '*Illiterate* him, I say, quite from your memory.'

Can you work out what Mrs Malaprop was really trying to say? (answers on page 24)

Hilda's 'muriel'

Have you seen my Muriel?
A modern-day Mrs Malaprop appeared for many years in the British television 'soap' *Coronation Street*, in the person of Hilda Ogden. She often referred to her 'Muriel' with great pride. But this was not her daughter, as you might expect. It was a scene painted on her living-room wall — a mural!

MALAPROPISMS

See if you can spot the malapropisms, or wrong words, in the following examples. You can use a dictionary to help. Perhaps you can suggest one or two of the right words. But don't worry if you can't. The answers are on pages 24 and 25. You might like to try them out on a friend or an adult.

1 The Spanish requisition.
2 Proliferation is the thief of time.
3 She received an anomalous letter.
4 I'm on the horns of a llama.
5 A mirage is an optical allusion.
6 The doctor said I had a congenial disorder.
7 The doctor gave me a subscription for ointment.
8 The models took lessons in deportation.
9 I wrote to the court for a conscript of the case.
10 He didn't need a backhand because he was amphibious.
11 He was vaccinated with an epidemic syringe.
12 The gymnast's display on the uneven bars was incredulous.
13 Calm down — don't get so historical.
14 He was fined for committing an illegible act.
15 She's at her wick's end.
16 He admired the church's flying buttocks.

The horns of a llama

Howlers

Howlers are glaring but amusing blunders that are closely related to malapropisms. The funniest are usually made by schoolchildren in essays and answers to exam questions:

1 Russia uses the acrylic alphabet.
2 Socrates died from an overdose of wedlock.
3 King George lay in state for two days in a catapult.
4 The practice of having only one wife is called monotony.
5 Pompeii was overcome by an overflow of red-hot saliva.

What should they have said? (answers on page 25)

PRONUNCIATION

2 Oops, I'll say that again

Not everyone says, or 'pronounces', words in the same way. Australians, Americans and Scots, for example, pronounce words in very different ways. Yet the language they all speak is called English. Even within the same country, there are hundreds of ways of speaking, called 'accents'. Everyone has an accent. Your accent depends on where you were brought up. No one accent is the correct way to speak. But it is easy to make mistakes when speaking, because in English not all words are pronounced as they are spelt.

English is difficult for a foreigner to learn because there are few rules of pronunciation that do not have several exceptions. Some consonants, such as 'c', 's' and 'g', have different sounds in different words. Sometimes, consonants are 'silent' — that is, not sounded at all — such as the 'k' in

Can you say what letters, if any, are silent in the following words? (answers on pages 25 and 26)
1 hymn
2 night
3 pneumatic
4 column
5 knitting
6 hearing
7 gnu
8 Saturday
9 hatch
10 fidget
11 Thomas
12 receipt
13 talk
14 wreath
15 dumb
16 psalm

6

PRONUNCIATION

'knee' and the 'g' in 'gnaw'. The 'h' at the beginning of some words is also silent, as in 'hour' and 'honest'.

Foreign people learning English have most difficulty with vowel sounds. And in English there is an alarmingly large range of vowel sounds with which the five symbols A E I O U have to cope. This mnemonic (aid to memory) phrase illustrates this range of English vowels: 'Who would know aught of art must learn, act, and then take his ease.' This contains fourteen vowel sounds — plus many dipthongs (two vowels pronounced as one syllable).

And if foreigners travel around English-speaking countries, they can become confused with the way vowel sounds change in different accents. The word 'bath', for example, is pronounced 'barth' in the south of England — that is, with a long 'a', as in 'farm'. In many other parts of Britain, it is pronounced with a short 'a', as in 'hat'. And in America, the 'a' is not quite as short and is pronounced as in the name 'Sam'.

I take it you already know
Of tough and bough and cough and dough?
Others may stumble, but not you,
On hiccough, thorough, lough and through.
Well done! And now you wish, perhaps,
To know of less familiar traps.
Beware of heard, a dreadful word,
That looks like beard and sounds like bird,
And dead: it's said like bed, not bead —
For goodness sake don't call it 'deed'!
Watch out for meat and great and threat
(They rhyme with suite and straight and debt).
A moth is not a moth in mother,
Nor both in bother, broth in brother,
And here is not a match for there,
Nor dear and fear for bear and pear,
And then there's dose and rose and lose —
Just look them up — and goose and choose,
And cork and work and card and ward,
And font and front and word and sword,
And do and go and thwart and cart —
Come, come, I've hardly made a start!
A dreadful language? Man alive!
I'd mastered it when I was five!

The group of English words that really stumps foreigners are those ending with '-ough'. Have a go at saying the following (answers on page 26):

bough	rough
cough	tough
dough	hiccough
enough	through
plough	thorough

Boughs bow

PRONUNCIATION

Emma Chisit?

Some time ago, the English writer Monica Dickens was signing copies of her latest book for customers of a bookshop in Sydney, Australia. When one woman, handing her a book, said 'Emma chisit', she wrote 'To Emma Chisit' inside the book, thinking that was the woman's name. But the woman was asking the price — Emma chisit? or 'How much is it?' As a result of this misunderstanding, a new 'language' was born — Strine. (Australian — geddit?)

Stress

Words may be split up into syllables. The word 'pet' has only one syllable. 'Silly' has two. A syllable is a 'unit of sound', and does not depend on the number of letters in a word. 'Any', for example, has two syllables (an-y), while 'strength' has only one.

Do you speak Strine?

People have fun with this Australian way of speaking, in which consonants are dropped and vowels mangled. See if you can translate the following Strine words and phrases (answers on page 26):

1 Pahn mee (clue, an apology)
2 Laze 'n gem (start of a speech)
3 Hip ride (top tunes)
4 Furry tiles (read to children at bed time)
5 Key powder vere (a warning)
6 Spin ear mitch (exact likeness)
7 Nouse mogen (a notice)
8 Grape leisure (much enjoyment)

When you say words of more than one syllable, you usually put the 'stress', or extra force, on one of them. 'Polite' is stressed on the second syllable — po-**lite**. 'Party' is stressed on the first — **par**-ty. With some words, different syllables are stressed depending on whether the word is a noun or a verb. For example, 'contest' is stressed on the first syllable as a noun — 'they entered the spelling **con**test' — but on the second as a verb — 'they decided to con**test** the

PRONUNCIATION

verdict'. The way you stress words may also depend on your accent. For example, 'yesterday' is usually stressed on the first syllable, but some people stress the last.

Wonder blunder
A word that is commonly mispronounced is 'wonder'. In Standard English (see page 31) it rhymes with 'thunder', but some people say it to rhyme with 'fonder'. In other words, they say 'wander' and 'wandering' for 'wonder' and 'wondering'. This could be confusing. It's an easy 'mistake' to make because of the spelling.

In ReceivedPronunciation (see page 31) the 'ou' vowel sound is usually pronounced as in 'round' — so bound, found, ground, hound, mound, pound and sound all rhyme. But there always seems to be an exception in English. What about 'wound'. With the meaning as in 'I wound up the clock,' it does rhyme with those words. But 'wound' meaning 'injury' rhymes with 'marooned'!

Try splitting the following words up into syllables (answers on page 26):

bitter
sight
wrong
champion
unusually
mispronunciation
artfulness
disestablishmentarianism

Same word, different sound
How do you say the word 'lead'? Well, there are two ways, depending on the meaning. The metal 'lead' is pronounced to rhyme with 'bed'. But if you 'lead' the way, you rhyme it with 'seed'. A common mistake is to confuse the metal spelling with the past tense of the verb 'lead', which is pronounced like the metal but is spelt 'led'.

The hound that found a mound

PRONUNCIATION

What about 'read'? This is an example of the present and past tenses of a verb spelt the same but pronounced differently. 'You now read (rhyming with seed) the paper every morning.' 'I read (rhyming with bed) the programme before I saw the play.'

the 'g' is soft, as in 'magic'. In 'finger', the 'g' is hard, as in 'good'. And in 'winger', the 'g' is almost 'swallowed', as in all words ending in 'ing', such as 'ending' or 'finding'.

Which type do the following words belong to, ranger, winger or finger? (answers page 27)

longer	danger
hanger	linger
ginger	stronger
stinger	clanger
banger	younger

Rangers' winger broke his finger

How do you sound the letter combination 'ng' in a word? Well, if you say 'Rangers' winger broke his finger', you've pronounced it in three different ways — provided you've said it correctly, that is. In 'Ranger',

See if you can pick out the exception, if any, in each of the following groups of words which look as if they all have the same sound: (answers on page 27)

1 root, boot, foot, hoot
2 post, host, lost, most
3 greed, bleed, deed, feed
4 cute, lute, brute, chute
5 laid, maid, paid, said
6 bead, bread, head, tread
7 cow, grow, mow, tow
8 brow, crow, how, now
9 brown gown, grown, town
10 tone, phone, one, bone
11 wood, food, hood, good
12 hear, near, wear, fear

10

PRONUNCIATION

'ello, 'ello, my name's Aitch!

Ghost letters

Common mistakes in pronunciation result from sounding letters that are not there — 'ghost' letters. People who worry about trying not to drop their 'h's often put one in at the beginning of a word that doesn't have one. When referring to the letter 'h' itself, many people say 'haitch'. But curiously enough the word is spelt 'aitch' — without an 'h'!

The word 'mischievous' has three syllables and is pronounced with the stress on the first one — **mis**-chie-vous. Many people insert an 'i' and pronounce it mis-***chie***-vi-ous, probably because many words do end in '-ious' — such as 'devious' and 'previous'.

Blunder of blunders

Few blunders can compare with one made by a famous radio announcer in an advertisement for a new dictionary. The dictionary was being sold in parts, with a new section on sale every week. With the first section came a free binder and a gramophone record on which this well-known broadcaster had recorded a message commending the dictionary to prospective purchasers. Unfortunately, when he was listing the special features, he referred to the 'pronounciation' guide — a common error, but he should have known the word is 'pronunciation'. And so should the people responsible for making the record.

If you can't beat them, join them

Pronunciation has changed over the years. English is spelt how it was pronounced in the Middle Ages, a few hundred years ago. For example, 'up' used to be pronounced as 'oop', 'out' as 'oot' and 'house' as 'hoose'. They are still pronounced this way in Scotland and parts of northern England. And these regional accents

PRONUNCIATION

are just as correct as Standard English (see page 31).

Some words start off being mispronounced because people are unfamiliar with them. A good example is the French word 'forte', meaning 'strong point', which is now widely used in English. It became confused with the musical term 'forte', which comes from Italian and means 'loud'. In Italian, the final 'e' in such words is always pronounced, so the musical term in English has two syllables and is pronounced 'for-tay'. But the French word 'forte' should really be pronounced as one syllable. If the French want to pronounce an 'e' at the end of a word, they put an accent on it ('forté'). Nevertheless, most people now say the word with two syllables. This 'mistake' is so widespread that anyone saying, for example, 'Spelling is not my *fort*' would be regarded as eccentric!

Pronunciation of surnames
Beauchamp   Beech'em
Beauclerc   Bo'clair
Beaulieu   Bew'ly
Belvoir   Beaver
Bicester   Bister
Chandos   Shandos
Chisholm   Chizum
Cholmondeley   Chumley
Cockburn   Co'burn
Colquhoun   Co'hoon
Fiennes   Fynes
Gough   Goff
Grosvenor   Gro'venor
Kirkby   Kirby
Maclean   Maclane
Mainwaring   Mannering
Marjoribanks   Marshbanks
Menzies   Mengis
Pepys   Peeps
Pugh   Pew
St John   Sinjun
Wemyss   Weems

PRONUNCIATION

**Can you pronounce these words properly?
(answers on page 28)**

Sandwich

1 advertisement
2 aegis
3 aesthetic
4 almond
5 alms
6 antipodes
7 antiquary
8 anemone
9 aristocrat
10 asinine
11 asphalt
12 ate
13 bathos
14 beige
15 boatswain
16 breeches
17 ceilidh
18 chaff
19 chameleon
20 chaos
21 chic
22 corps

23 coxswain
24 dais
25 depot
26 dour
27 dynasty
28 eisteddfod
29 epitome
30 exacerbate
31 falcon
32 forehead
33 Gaelic
34 gunwale
35 handkerchief
36 heir
37 hiccough
38 hyperbole
39 idyll
40 inchoate
41 indict
42 kilometer
43 kosher
44 laity
45 lichen
46 lieu
47 macabre
48 macho
49 maestro
50 mauve
51 medieval
52 migraine
53 missile
54 mortgage
55 nadir
56 niche
57 oestrogen
58 often
59 orgy
60 paucity
61 parabola

62 pathos
63 pejorative
64 pergola
65 personnel
66 phlegm
67 piquant
68 plait
69 plethora
70 posthumous
71 primarily
72 pseudonym
73 psyche
74 qualm
75 quay
76 rabbi
77 route
78 recipe
79 reggae
80 sanguine
81 scimitar
82 segue
83 seismic
84 senile
85 sheikh
86 simile
87 status
88 succinct
89 taciturn
90 triptych
91 vaccinate
92 vehemence
93 venison
94 veterinary
95 victuals
96 viscid
97 viscount
98 vitiate
99 xylophone
100 zealot

Quay

SLIPS OF THE TONGUE

3 Don't mention the wart!

People sometimes say something by mistake that gives away what they are thinking or perhaps reveals how they feel. Schoolchildren might make fun of a teacher's beard in private, and then find themselves calling him 'Mr Beard' to his face.

Imagine the embarrassment if a teacher with a large wart on his nose suddenly reappeared after being away with a cold. A colleague, inquiring about his health, and trying not to look at the wart might easily slip up and ask: 'How's your wart today?' This kind of blunder is more a slip of the mind than of the tongue. It is called a 'Freudian slip' after the famous Austrian psychologist Sigmund Freud. He was a doctor who studied people's minds. No matter how hard you try to hide your thoughts, you might still say something that gives the game away.

This often happens to people who tell lies. A person at work who had been allowed an afternoon off to go to a 'relative's funeral' might be asked next day by the boss: 'How many turned up?' The answer 'ten thousand' would give away the fact that he or she had gone to a sports event rather than a cemetery.

There was the sad case of the editor of an Old Boy's magazine, who had kept it going for over twenty years. He lost the sight of an eye in an accident, and this, combined with poor health and his age, meant that he would probably not be able to continue producing the magazine. The headline in the local newspaper unfortunately read: End in sight for Old Boy's magazine.

See if you can spot the Freudian slip in the following wedding invitation (answer on page 27):
'Mr and Mrs Brown request the honour of your presents at the marriage of their daughter ...'

SPOONERISMS

4 The cat that popped on its drawers and other word mix-ups

If you are feeling cold, why not fight a liar? Or you might shake a tower when you are hot and bothered. If that makes sense to you, you will probably know the difference between a lion sitting on a thorn and a thundercloud — one roars with pain, the other pours with rain. All these are examples of spoonerisms — switching the first sounds of two words. So 'fight a liar' is 'light a fire' and 'shake a tower' is 'take a shower'.

People sometimes make up spoonerisms for fun, as in the 'what's the difference between' riddles. Try this one: What's the difference between a jeweller and a jailer? (answer on page 27).

Spoonerisms are called after the Reverend William Archibald Spooner, the warden of New College, Oxford, in the early 1900s. He was well known for mixing up his words in this way, and was often embarrassed by some of the things he accidentally came out with. He once gave out a hymn in chapel as 'Kinquering Congs' (Conquering Kings). Also in chapel, he is said to have complained: 'Someone is occupewing my pie' (occupying my pew), and he once asked a student to 'form up a fill', completely swapping the words around.

Spooner also went round Oxford on a 'well-boiled icicle' (a well-oiled bicycle). He is said to have scolded a wayward student with these remarks: 'Sir, you have tasted a whole worm. You have hissed my mystery lectures. You will leave Oxford by the town drain.'
(answers on page 27)

Shake a tower

15

SPOONERISMS

Tasting a whole worm

The vowel sounds have been changed in the following piece. See if you can decipher it:
'Gid moaning Who or ye toady?'
'Aim phone. A biked oh coke fir year ground feather. Well Hugh Luke et?'
'Poor hops. Bet horse list earl has tooth.'

By the way, did you hear the one about the cat that jumped off the wall? It popped on its drawers!

(answers on page 27)

The cat popped on its drawers

Be wary of words

Words can play tricks. You need to have your wits about you and to think logically.
Here are some examples to test your 'lateral thinking' (answers on page 27):

1 Two Americans met to have lunch. One was the father of the other's son. How were they related to each other?

2 It is a well-known fact that eating too many hard-boiled eggs can make you constipated. Can you say how many hard-boiled eggs it is safe for a hungry man to eat on an empty stomach?

3 A man and his wife have seven sons, and every one of the sons has a sister. How many are there altogether in the family?

4 'There is three mistakes in this sentance.' Can you spot them?

5 A plane crashed in the jungle. Where did they bury the survivors?

6 What is the next letter in this series:
O T T F F S S

5 Statements that don't follow what was said before

A newspaper account of a court case in which a bakery was being prosecuted reported that: 'Mrs Rathbone bought the loaf from a supermarket and spotted the inch-wide piece of metal before eating it.' You'd think that, having spotted the offending object, she might have avoided swallowing it. Perhaps she did not have enough iron in her diet!

We know what the newspaper was trying to say — she might have eaten the metal if she had not spotted it. It is easy enough to make such gaffes in speech, but you would expect an editor to stop them getting into print.

Similarly, a sports reporter announced that a show-jumper 'is better after being kicked in the head by her horse'. This was just an unfortunate choice of word. Substitute 'recovering' for 'better' and there's no problem. 'Better' implies that the kick in the head did her good!

A decorating and general repairs company advertised: 'Difficult job needs doing in the house? Don't kill your husband. We'll do it for you.' What they meant, of course, was that they would do the job — not kill the husband. In truth, there's no confusion here. We know exactly what they mean, but it can sound funny when people mix up ideas in this way.

Cause and effect

A cricketer explaining why he had not been playing very well for a spell said: 'I hurt my thumb and then, obviously, the mother-in-law died.'

I hurt my thumb ...

This sounds as if his mother-in-law died because he hurt his thumb. What he meant was that he lost his form for two separate reasons: first, the accident to his thumb; second, a death in the family. He used the word 'obviously' because, in his mind, it was obvious that the death of a close relative would upset him and affect his form.

Such slips of the tongue are called by a Latin term — *non sequiturs*. It means something that does not logically follow what has gone before.

NON SEQUITURS

Here are some non sequiturs taken from essays on famous people. See if you can say why they are non sequiturs (answers on page 29):

1 The Austrian composer Haydn: His last visitor was an officer of the French army occupying Vienna, who carried the old man to the piano. Haydn died a few days later.

2 The Dutch artist Hobbema: He was appointed city wine inspector at Amsterdam, where he had been born. He did little painting after his appointment.

3 The English writer Thackeray: He concealed his identity by using absurd names, such as 'Michael Angelo Titmarsh'. His wife became insane in 1840.

4 The German philosopher Nietzsche: He attracted little attention before he became insane in 1889, but later influenced many major German and French philosophers, poets and psychologists.

Red, White and Rosé ...

NON SEQUITURS

Leaving things dangling

'Looking down from the helicopter, the people in the street seemed like ants.' This is a common mistake. It would be correct to say: 'As seen from the helicopter, the people ...' But when you use a word like 'looking' in this way, someone has to do the looking. And it certainly wasn't the people in the street.

Here's another example: 'While riding his bike, a dog chased him.' Well, unless the dog was riding his bike, this is a similar blunder. When you use an '-ing' word, or 'participle', in this way, it must be related to the person doing it: 'While riding his bike, he was chased by a dog.' Or you could say: 'While he was riding his bike, a dog chased him.' When these '-ing' endings are related to the wrong 'doer', they are called 'misrelated' participles.

Sometimes the participles are not related to a 'doer' at all, as in 'Not being hungry, it would be a waste of money going to the restaurant.' In this sentence, 'being' is unrelated. No one is doing the 'being'. In other words, it is left dangling.

Can you correct these sentences (and the above)?
(answers on page 29):

Fooling around in class, the teacher gave her detention.

Acting on a tip-off, the robbers were caught in the act.

On hearing the exam results, there were wild celebrations in our house.

Having saved up all winter, it was now possible to buy a bike.

Here's a similar blunder, but not with an '-ing' word:

Faced with gunfire from all sides, it was pointless to continue the fight.

Tally-ho!

ANTICLIMAX

6 What a big let-down

'Hurricane Charlie swept in from the coast leaving a trail of devastation: Millions of dollars' worth of damage was done, thousands of people were left homeless, 132 people were injured, six are missing, believed drowned, and typewriters were knocked off desks.'

This comes from a news report of a natural disaster. It is an example of 'anticlimax'. Ideas that seem to be leading up to the most important are made ridiculous by keeping the least important till last.

It is the opposite of 'climax', where you build up ideas to make a powerful point or to crown an argument — as in 'I came, I saw, I conquered.'

Anticlimax may be used for comic effect — as in 'I came, I saw, I caught a cold.' Comedians use it in this way: 'The secret of staying young is to live honestly, eat slowly and lie about your age.'

Here are three well-known quotations — the first from Shakespeare's King Henry V, the second from Winston Churchill's war speeches, and the third from a speech by American President Abraham Lincoln. They have been changed to produce anticlimax. Can you restore the word or phrase that has been substituted in each case?

1 Follow your spirit; and, upon this charge, cry 'God for Harry! England and Saint Michael!'

2 Never in the field of human conflict was so much owed by so many to the humble potato.

3 You can fool all the people some of the time, and some of the people all the time, but you can not make a horse drink water.

(answers on page 29)

WEASEL WORDS

7 So what — it's quite meaningless!

It is said that statistics can prove anything. Certainly, all sorts of people and organizations use them, or misuse them, for their own benefit — especially politicians, advertisers and salespeople. Often, this is possible by clever use of language. But sometimes they can fool themselves.

A magazine recently sent out thousands of letters in an effort to persuade people to take out a regular subscription. In it was the proud boast that 'four out of five of our long-term subscribers renew every year'. 'So what!' to that. It doesn't take an Einstein to work out that one in every five did not renew. In other words, if the magazine had 20,000 long-term subscribers, it would lose 4,000 of them when it was time to renew. Put like that, it doesn't sound too good. In fact, the situation sounds pretty desperate, for at that rate, if they did not get any new subscribers, they would be down to about 10,000 in just three years.

Here's an example from an atlas. The Fascinating Facts section about one country included this piece of information: 'Nearly 70 per cent of the people live in the northern two-thirds of the country.' Maybe you can say what's remarkable about this (answer on page 29).

What about this quote? 'Statistics show that of those who form the habit of eating, none survive.' Does this make any sense to you?

The television comic Benny Hill worked out a good ruse: 'The odds against there being a bomb on a plane are a million to one, and against two bombs a billion to one. So next time you fly, cut the odds and take a bomb.'

Can you spot the flaw in the following argument?

A lemon is a yellow fruit.
That fruit is yellow.
So that fruit must be a lemon.

21

IDIOMS

8 That's not what I meant

The English language is full of traps for the unwary — as a cricket commentator discovered when he made this remark: 'Well, listeners, since you were last with us, Richards decided to chance his arm and it came off.' This is perfectly good English, but it sounds like poor Richards lost his arm. The reason for this is that the commentator was using 'idioms' — phrases that have come to have a special meaning that cannot be worked out from the words themselves.

Chancing your arm ...

To 'chance your arm' means to 'boldly take a risk'. And if something 'comes off' it 'is successful'. So Richards batted boldly, risked being out, but succeeded in making a lot of runs. And he still had both his arms!

A chat show host on television once introduced a British cabinet minister with the words: 'I think he's doing an appalling job.' What he meant to say was that his guest's post — minister for Northern Ireland — was a terrible job to have to do. But it came out as if he was accusing the minister of doing his job badly.

A woman worried about her cat staying out all night rang the radio vet and said: 'I went out early to put the rubbish out for the dustman and found him soaking wet and cowering under a bush.' Yes, you've got it — she meant her wet cat.

The 'dangling participles' we referred to earlier (page 19) can also conjure up very strange pictures: 'Turning the corner, the supermarket came into view.' Have you ever seen a supermarket turn a corner?
See if you can spot the 'impossible' in this report of a pop group touring a small country in eastern Europe (answer on page 30):
'The coach driver drove wildly but well, with her fingers continually on the horn, waving the narrow streets clear with one hand and proudly drawing attention to her famous passengers with the other.'

HOMOPHONES

9 Sounds the same to me!

Words that have the same sound but different spellings are called 'homophones'. An example of a pair of homophones is wine (a drink) and whine (to grumble). There are many of these pairs (or triples or more) in English, which makes it more difficult for foreigners to understand.

Wrong words have been used in the following sentences.
See if you can find the correct homophone in each case.
(answers on page 30)

1. She had trouble carrying her double-base.
2. To many cooks spoil the broth.
3. He's so vein.
4. The bride lifted her vale.
5. Orange peal is used in marmalade.
6. Prays the Lord and pass the ammunition.
7. The prints of darkness arrived.
8. She told a tail of a sad donkey.
9. Hear we are again.
10. Pink string and ceiling wax.
11. Someone called last-knight to canvas my vote.
12. This is the finest plaice for fish and chips.
13. I chews what I eat for breakfast.
14. I guest how many people came to stay.
15. The son is shining.
16. The boat shop had a closing-down sail.
17. I'm board with playing chess.
18. A heard of cattle thundered over the plain.
19. She met her friend at the fate.
20. I mist classes because of the thick fog.

Fun with homophones (answers on page 31):

1. Would you say naval operations are conducted by a surgeon or an admiral?

2. I listen to a cereal regularly at eight o'clock. Is that possible?

3. See how many wrong homophones you can find in this sentence: Before the crews, there cases were taken strait to the bridle sweet.

4. Use one pair of homophones to complete each of the following correctly:

A I can undo my own laces, so long as they're … in a ….

B The big bad wolf … until he was … in the face.

C Jack's … up the … stalk twice today.

Answers

1 What Mrs Malaprop meant to say (page 4)

1 *She's as headstrong as an alligator on the banks of the Nile.*
2 *Obliterate him, I say, quite from your memory.*

Malapropisms (page 5)

1 *Inquisition — the Spanish Inquisition was a special court set up to punish people who disagreed with the Church's teachings. (Not requisition — a formal request, or a written order to send supplies.)*
2 *Procrastination — putting off doing things. (Not proliferation — a rapid increase in numbers.)*
3 *Anonymous — not giving a name. (Not anomalous — irregular or abnormal.)*
4 *Dilemma — a choice between two equally unpleasant decisions. (Not llama — a South American animal.)*
5 *Illusion — an image that gives the wrong impression. (Not allusion — an indirect reference to something.)*
6 *Congenital — existing from birth. (Not congenial — pleasant or agreeable.)*
7 *Prescription — a written order for a medicine. (Not subscription — a membership fee, or money paid for issues of a magazine.)*
8 *Deportment — the way you walk or move. (Not deportation — expulsion of someone from a country.)*
9 *Transcript — an official copy of the proceedings. (Not conscript — someone who has to enlist for military service.)*
10 *Ambidextrous — able to use either hand equally well. (Not amphibious able to live on land or in water.)*
11 *Hypodermic — for use under the skin. (Not epidemic — a sudden and widespread outbreak of a disease.)*
12 *Incredible — hard to believe. (Not incredulous — not believing something.)*
13 *Hysterical — uncontrollably excited. (Not historical — associated with history.)*
14 *Illegal — against the law. (Not illegible — unreadable.)*
15 *Wit's end — the end of your endurance. (Not wick's end – a wick burns in a candle or oil lamp.)*

16 *Buttress — a support built to the outside of a wall. (Not buttocks — the fleshy parts of your bottom!)*

An amphibious serve

Did you spot any of the right words? If you got more than two, give yourself a pat on the back. Five or more and you're a genie (or should that be 'genius'?)

Howlers
1 *Cyrillic — the alphabet introduced to Russia by St Cyril. (Not acrylic, an artificial fibre.)*
2 *Hemlock — a poison. (Not wedlock which means marriage.)*
3 *Catafalque — a platform on which a coffin is laid. (Not catapult, which is a weapon used for firing stones.)*
4 *Monogamy — having only one wife. (Not monotony, which means boring.)*
5 *Lava — the hot material thrown out by volcanoes. (Not saliva, which is spit.)*

2 Oops, I'll say that again
Silent letters (page 6)
The letters in bold type are silent:
  1 *hym**n***
  2 *nig**h**t*
  3 ***p**neumatic*
  4 *colum**n***
  5 ***k**nitting*
  6 *hearing (none silent)*
  7 ***g**nu*
  8 *Saturday (none silent)*
  9 *ha**t**ch (although the 't' is not sounded, it makes the 'ch' into a 'hard' sound, as in*

'chips', rather than as in 'chute')
10 fi**d**get (the 'd' makes the 'g' 'soft', as in 'page', rather than as in 'get')
11 **Th**omas (the 'th' is pronounced as a 't')
12 recei**p**t
13 ta**l**k
14 **w**reath
15 dum**b**
16 **p**sa**l**m (pronounced 'sarm', with both 'p' and 'l' silent)

Were you stumped? (page 7)

bough and **plough** are both pronounced to rhyme with 'cow'.
cough rhymes with 'scoff',
dough with 'low'.
enough, **rough** and **tough** rhyme with 'puff'.
hiccough rhymes with 'pick-up.'
through rhymes with 'crew'.
thorough rhymes with 'kookaburra'.

Do you speak strine? (page 8)

1 *pahn mee* — pardon me
2 *laze 'n gem* — ladies and gentlemen
3 *hip ride* — hit parade
4 *furry tiles* — fairytales
5 *key powder vere* — keep out of here
6 *spin ear mitch* — spitting image
7 *nouse mogen* — no smoking
8 *grape leisure* — great pleasure

Split syllables (page 9)

bitter (2 syllables, *bit-ter*)
sight (1)
wrong (1)
champion (3, *cham-pi-on*)
unusually (5, *un-u-su-al-ly*)
mispronunciation (6, *mis-pro-nun-ci-a-tion*),
artfulness (3, *art-ful-ness*)
disestablishmentarianism (9, *dis-est-ab-lish-ment-ar-i-an-ism*)

The winger's finger (page 10)

Longer, linger, stronger and younger are in the finger 'group'.

Hanger, **stinger**, **clanger** and **banger** *are said like winger.*
Ginger and *Danger* have soft 'g's, like ranger.

Odd ones out (page 10)

1 *foot* (a shorter vowel sound)
2 *lost* (shorter sound)
3 all have the same sound
4 *cute* (a 'you' rather than an 'oo' sound)
5 *said* (rhymes with 'bed')
6 *bead* (rhymes with 'seed')
7 *cow* (rhymes with 'now')
8 *crow* (rhymes with 'toe')
9 *grown* (rhymes with 'moan')
10 *one* (rhymes with 'fun')
11 *food* (long vowel sound)
12 *wear* (rhymes with 'hair')

Did you pronounce the words properly? (page 13) see page 28 for answers

3 Don't mention the wart! (page 14)

The invitation should have read: 'Mr and Mrs Brown request the honour of your **presence** *at the marriage of ...'*

4 The cat that popped on its drawers (pages 15 and 16)

The difference between a jeweller and a jailer — one sells watches and the other watches cells.

What Dr Spooner meant to say

You have wasted a whole term. You have missed my history lectures. You will leave Oxford by the down train.

'Good morning. How are you today?' 'I'm fine. I baked a cake for your grandfather. Will he like it?' 'Perhaps. But he's lost all his teeth.'

The cat dropped on its paws.

Be wary of words (page 16)

1 *They were husband and wife. Most people first think that 'two Americans' refers to two men. If this were the case, the problem would be impossible. You have to get away from your 'logical' line of thought to solve it.*

2 *A person cannot eat more than one egg on an empty stomach. After that, the person's stomach is no longer empty!*

3 *Ten. There is one daughter, who is a sister to all seven sons, so 8*

Did you pronounce these words properly*? (page 13)

1 advertisement ad-**vert**-iz-ment
2 aegis **ee**-jiss
3 aesthetic **ees**-thet-ic
4 almond the 'l' is silent
5 alms the 'l' is silent
6 antipodes an-**tip**-oh-dees
7 antiquary **ant**-tik-war-ee
8 anemone a-**nem**-uh-nee
9 aristocrat **a**-ris-toe-crat
10 asinine **ass**-ih-nine
11 asphalt **as**-felt or as-falt
12 ate et is more usual than ayt
13 bathos **bay**-thos
14 beige bayj
15 boatswain **bo**-sun
16 breeches rhymes with 'pitches'
17 ceilidh **kay**-lih
18 chaff rhymes with 'staff'
19 chameleon kee-**meel**-yun
20 chaos **kay**-oss
21 chic sheek
22 corps kor
23 coxswain **kok**-sun
24 dais **day**iss or dace
25 depot **depp**-o
26 dour rhymes with 'poor'
27 dynasty **din**-us-tee
28 eisteddfod ey-**steth**-vod or es-teth-vod
29 epitome ih-**pit**-uh-mee
30 exacerbate eg-**zass**-uh-bate
31 falcon **fawl**-kun
32 forehead **for**-id or **for**-hed
33 Gaelic **gay**-lik or **gal**-ik
34 gunwale **gun**-uhl
35 handkerchief **hang**-ker-chiff
36 heir air
37 hiccough **hik**-up
38 hyperbole hy-**per**-boh-lee
39 idyll **id**-ill
40 inchoate in-**ko**-ayt
41 indict in-**dite**
42 kilometer **kil**-uh-meet-ur or ki-**lom**-it-ur
43 kosher **ko**-shuh
44 laity **lay**-i-tee
45 lichen as liken or to rhyme with 'kitchen'
46 lieu lee-**you** or loo
47 macabre ma-**ka**-bruh
48 macho **match**-oh or **mak**-oh
49 maestro **my**-stroh
50 mauve to rhymes with 'stove'

51 medieval med-ih-**ee**-vul
52 migraine **mee**-grain or **my**-grain
53 missile **miss**-ile
54 mortgage **mor**-gij
55 nadir **nay**-deer
56 niche nitch or neesh
57 oestrogen **ee**-str-jen
58 often **off**-en
59 orgy **or**-jee
60 paucity **paw**-sit-ee
61 parabola puh-**rab**-uh-la
62 pathos **pay**-thoss
63 pejorative pi-**jorr**-at-iv
64 pergola **per**-gul-uh
65 personnel per-suhn-**ell**
66 phlegm flem
67 piquant **pee**-kuhnt
68 plait plat
69 plethora **pleth**-er-uh
70 posthumous silent 'h': **pos**-tyou-muss
71 primarily **pry**-mar-ih-lee
72 pseudonym **sue**-duh-nim
73 psyche **sy**-kee
74 qualm silent 'l': kwahm
75 quay kee
76 rabbi **rab**-by
77 route root
78 recipe **res**-ip-ee
79 reggae **reg**-gay
80 sanguine **sang**-win
81 scimitar **sim**-it-uh
82 segue **seg**-way
83 seismic **size**-mik
84 senile **seen**-ile
85 sheikh shake
86 simile **sim**-ih-lee
87 status **stay**-tuss
88 succinct the cc as in success
89 taciturn **tass**-ih-turn
90 triptych **trip**-tik
91 vaccinate **vak**-sin-ayt
92 vehemence the 'h' is silent
93 venison 's' as in hiss
94 veterinary **vet**-rin-ree
95 victuals rhymes with 'skittles'
96 viscid **viss**-id
97 viscount the 's' is silent: **vy**-kount
98 vitiate **vish**-ih-ayt
99 xylophone **zy**-luh-fohn
100 zealot **zel**-ut

* Using Received Pronunciation (see page 31)

children and 2 adults make 10.

4 *'There is ...' (rather than 'there are') is one.*
'Sentance' (sentence) is two and the third mistake is that there are only two!

5 *You don't bury survivors!*

6 *The next letter in the line is E. The letters are initial letters of words — the numbers one, two, three, and so on.*

5 Statements that don't follow (page 18)
Non sequiturs: *The way the sentences are worded, it would appear:*
1 *that Haydn died because the soldier carried him to his piano,*
2 *that Hobbema stopped painting because he was too busy drinking,*
3 *that Thackeray's wife went mad because of the silly names he used for himself*
4 *and that Nietzsche influenced other writers only because he became insane.*
In a funny way, all these conclusions could be true!

Dangling participles (page 19)
The following answers are not the only correct ones:
As we (or whoever) are not hungry, it would be a waste of money going to the restaurant.
The teacher gave her detention for fooling around in class.
Acting on a tip-off, the police caught the robbers in the act.
When we heard the exam results, there were wild celebrations in our house.
Having saved up all winter, I (or whoever) could now buy a bike.
With gunfire coming from all sides, it was pointless to continue the fight.
or
Faced with gunfire from all sides, they realized it was pointless to continue the fight.

6 What a big let-down (page 20)
1 *Follow your spirit; and, upon this charge, cry 'God for Harry! England and Saint **George!**'*
2 *Never in the field of human conflict was so much owed by so many to **so few.***
3 *You can fool all the people some of the time, and some of the people all the time, but you can not **fool all the people all of the time.***

7 So what! (page 21)
There is nothing remarkable about nearly 70 per cent of the people living in two-thirds of

the country — two-thirds is nearly 70 per cent. Now if 70 per cent of the people lived in one third, that would be worth remarking on.

'Statistics show that of those who form the habit of eating, none survive'. This is a spoof, and nothing to do with statistics. We all form the habit of eating, and we all have to die some time!

The statement about a lemon does not say it is the only yellow fruit. The fruit referred to might be a lemon, but, of course, it could also be a banana.

8 That's not what I meant (page 22)

Not only did the coach driver have no hands on the wheel, if this report was true, but she would have needed three hands to (1) keep her fingers on the horn, (2) wave the streets clear with one hand and (3) draw attention with the other.

9 Sounds the same to me! (page 23)

1 *She had trouble carrying her double-**bass**.*
2 ***Too*** *many cooks spoil the broth.*
3 *He's so **vain**.*
4 *The bride lifted her **veil**.*
5 *Orange **peel** is used in marmalade.*
6 ***Praise*** *the Lord and pass the ammunition.*
7 *The **prince** of darkness arrived.*
8 *She told a **tale** of a sad donkey.*
9 ***Here*** *we are again.*
10 *Pink string and **sealing** wax.*
11 *Someone called last **night** to **canvass** my vote.*
12 *This is the finest **place** for fish and chips.*
13 *I **choose** what I eat for breakfast.*
14 *I **guessed** how many people came to stay.*
15 *The **sun** is shining.*
16 *The boat shop had a closing-down **sale**.*
17 *I'm **bored** with playing chess.*
18 *A **herd** of cattle thundered over the plain.*
19 *She met her friend at the **fête**.*
20 *I **missed** classes because of the thick fog.*

Fun with homophones

1 *An admiral would conduct **naval** operations, although a surgeon might be concerned with someone's **navel**, or 'belly-button'.*

2 *You would listen to a **serial** (a continuing story) on a regular basis, but you would only listen to a **cereal** if it was of the 'snap, crackle and pop' kind!*

3 *Before the **cruise, their** cases were taken **straight** to the **bridal suite**.*

4A *I can undo my own laces, so long as they're **not** in a **knot**.*

4B *The big bad wolf **blew** until he was **blue** in the face.*

4C *Jack's **been** up the **bean** stalk twice today.*

> Standard English is the speech or 'dialect' of the upper and upper-middle classes. It is normally used in writing English and teaching it to foreigners.

> **RP — Received Pronunciation** — is the pronunciation of that variety of English widely considered to be least regional, being originally that used by the educated people in southern England. RP is a neutral, national standard.

The three-handed coach driver